After Goldilocks

story by Johanna Richard

illustrations by
Dennis Hockerman

HARCOURT BRACE & COMPANY

Orlando Atlanta Austin Boston San Francisco Chicago Dallas New York
Toronto London

Three bowls of soup?
"Not mine," said Baby Bear.

Three soft chairs?
"Not mine," said Baby Bear.

Three sleepy heads?
"Not mine," said Baby Bear.

Three quiet beds?
"Not mine," said Baby Bear.

Three good nights.